What Happens in a Skyscraper

by Arthur Shay

REILLY & LEE BOOKS • CHICAGO

Other Arthur Shay books in the series:

WHAT HAPPENS AT A NEWSPAPER

WHAT HAPPENS AT A TELEVISION STATION

WHAT HAPPENS AT THE CIRCUS

WHAT HAPPENS AT THE LIBRARY

WHAT HAPPENS AT THE ZOO

WHAT HAPPENS IN A CAR FACTORY

WHAT HAPPENS WHEN YOU BUILD A HOUSE

WHAT HAPPENS WHEN YOU GO TO THE HOSPITAL

WHAT HAPPENS WHEN YOU MAIL A LETTER

WHAT HAPPENS WHEN YOU MAKE A TELEPHONE CALL

WHAT HAPPENS WHEN YOU PUT MONEY IN THE BANK

WHAT HAPPENS WHEN YOU SPEND MONEY

WHAT HAPPENS WHEN YOU TRAVEL BY PLANE

This book is for my daughter Lauren,
my favorite Hancock tenant

Cartoon by Jay Lynch

Published by Reilly & Lee Books, a division of Henry Regnery Company
114 West Illinois Street, Chicago, Illinois 60610
Library of Congress Catalog Card Number: 72-183834
Manufactured in the United States of America

To Parents and Teachers

When I was ten and growing up in New York, my father took me downtown to "watch the tallest building in the world going up." Since then—whether I am flying into La Guardia Airport or driving to Manhattan from New Jersey—whenever I see the Empire State Building, I always remember that gold and blue day in the thirties when my father, full of immigrant awe of the works of America, introduced me to history in the making.

A few years ago I took my own ten-year-old, Steve, to see the John Hancock Center rising on Michigan Avenue in Chicago. Thinking of my son's delight and my father's awe, I tried to sort out my own feelings about skyscrapers: I love them, for they are lofty dreams brought to life by man in peaceful command of his technical skills.

As I write, two more skyscrapers, a few stories taller than the Empire State and the Hancock, have just been finished in New York. A couple of miles from the Hancock, the Sears Building is soaring upward, destined (at least for a while) to be the tallest in the world. However, the Hancock is unique: along with its 400 business tenants, it contains some 700 apartments. People *live* there!

As I photographed "Big John," I soon realized that my subject was a city within a city. As is the case when I photograph any metropolis, my coverage was necessarily selective. I show the supermarket and pool on the forty-fourth floor but not the sauna or laundry rooms. I show the window washers at work but not the equally essential electricians or janitors.

I hope that adults using this book will guide their youngsters to an awareness of the problems—and potential—of city life. What are the advantages of a building like the Hancock? What factors did the building's designers have to consider? If the children were to design their own skyscrapers, what features would they add to those of the Hancock—or change?

Arthur Shay

The John Hancock Center, in Chicago, is one of the tallest buildings in the world. It is 100 stories high, and 1,456 feet from the sidewalk to the tips of the two TV towers at the top of the building. That's just about four and a half football fields high! Sometimes when you look up at "Big John" (the Hancock's nickname) from the ground, you can't see the top, which is often hidden by clouds or fog.

More than 10,000 people work at, live in, or visit Big John every day. As you will see, the John Hancock Center is really a city within a city.

FLOORS 98 TO 100 AND 43 HOUSE THE MECHANICAL AND AIR CONDITIONING EQUIPMENT FOR THE BUILDING AS WELL AS ELEVATOR MACHINERY.
UNH!
A GOURMET RESTAURANT IS LOCATED ON FLOORS 95 AND 96.
GASTON! DO YOU SERVE CRABS HERE?
WE SERVE ANYBODY, SIR.
MENU
FLOORS 45 THROUGH 92 HAVE 705 APARTMENTS.
!
YUM!
BUILDING RESIDENTS OFTEN VISIT THE SAUNA BATH AND POOL ON THE 44TH FLOOR.
THANKS, PAL!
I'LL GET A BIRD'S-EYE SHOT OF THIS BUILDING!
LOOKS LIKE THIS BULB IS NO GOOD.
RATTLE RATTLE.
!
THAT CROWN OF LIGHTS IS FOR THE BIRDS!
I'VE LEAPED TALL BUILDINGS AT A SINGLE BOUND BEFORE, BUT THIS IS RIDICULOUS!
?
LOOKS LIKE RAIN.
ONLY 10,000 MORE WINDOWS TO GO. THEN WE CAN BREAK FOR LUNCH!
GREETINGS, EARTHLING!
HI, I'M LAUREN SHAY.
YUM!
JUNIOR! YOU FORGOT YOUR LUNCH AGAIN!
IT'S A LIVING.
!
TELEVISION AND RADIO COMMUNICATIONS EQUIPMENT IS LOCATED ON FLOORS 93 AND 97.
!
77
78
79
80
THE OBSERVATORY ON THE 94TH FLOOR IS OPEN TO THE PUBLIC.
NUMBER 88 IS WINNING THE RACE IN INDIANAPOLIS!
IT'S RAINING IN MICHIGAN!
SURF'S UP IN LOS ANGELES!
RESIDENTS OF THE BUILDING DO THEIR GROCERY SHOPPING IN THE SUPER-MARKET ON THE 44TH FLOOR.
THIS IS THE WORLD'S HIGHEST SUPERMARKET, I'LL BET!
YES, BUT THE PRICES ARE LOW!
MANY ADVERTISING AGENCIES ARE LOCATED IN THE BUILDING. FLOORS 13 THROUGH 41 INCLUDE ONE MILLION SQUARE FEET OF MODERN OFFICE SPACE.
WE JUST GOT THE SUDZO DETERGENT ACCOUNT, J.B.
GREAT B.J., WE'LL CLEAN UP!

INTERESTING EXHIBITIONS ARE PROVIDED IN THE MEZZANINE.
I DON'T GO FOR THIS MODERN ART.
LOCATED BELOW STREET LEVEL, THESE SNACK SHOPS OFFER FAST SERVICE.
SPECIAL
SOUP-FRANKS-ETC.-
ZIP!
EATS
THIS IS AN ELEVATING EXPERIENCE.
YOU KNOW MISTER BRICHTA, I LIVE UP ON THE 62ND FLOOR; I WORK HERE ON THE 39TH FLOOR; WE SHOP ON THE 1ST FLOOR... COME TO THINK OF IT I HAVEN'T BEEN OUTSIDE THIS BUILDING FOR YEARS!
YOU MEAN THERE'S SOMETHING OUTSIDE OF THIS BUILDING, MISTER BAKER ?!
TICK TICK TICK
FOR REALLY HIGH FASHION WE MAY MOVE TO THE 91ST FLOOR!
BOUTIQUE
AW MA...
I'M GLAD THE BANK IS ON THE FIRST FLOOR. I'M SCARED OF HEIGHTS!
BANK
OUCH! THIS ICE IS ARTIFICIAL, BUT IT HURTS LIKE THE REAL THING!
HEADQUARTERS FOR THE INSTITUTE OF FOREIGN STUDIES IS ON THE 15TH FLOOR.
WOW!
THE EIFFEL TOWER!
ONLY ONE PET IS ALLOWED ON EACH RESIDENTIAL FLOOR.
A POSTAL STATION IS LOCATED IN THE BASEMENT, BELOW STREET LEVEL.
HOW MANY DAYS DOES IT TAKE FOR A LETTER TO GET TO THE 88TH FLOOR?

This is how the 104,000-square-foot site of Big John looked when construction began. Inside the Hancock Center are 2,800,000 square feet of space.

It took only three years to erect the Hancock Center, but hundreds of people planned Big John for another three years *before* the builders went to work. A model of the Hancock shows how much taller Big John is than its neighboring skyscrapers.

In its front yard, just below street level, the Hancock Center has an outdoor ice skating rink, which is open to the public in the winter. Tons of copper refrigeration pipes are buried under the rink to keep the ice from melting when the temperature gets above freezing. In the summer the refrigeration is turned off, and the skating rink becomes a lovely pond.

People who drive to the Hancock Center can leave their cars at the rear of the building. Attendants drive the cars up a winding ramp and park them between the sixth and the twelfth floors – seven floors of garage. Naturally there's a spiral "down" ramp for cars leaving the building.

More than 100,000 letters and parcels arrive at Big John every day. Trucks deliver packages and mail to the postal station in the basement.

The lower lobbies and hallways are called concourses. Along the Hancock's concourses are a gift shop, a bank, a stationery store, a drugstore, and a cafeteria. David Hansen runs a barbershop during the week; the shop becomes a school for hair stylists on Sunday.

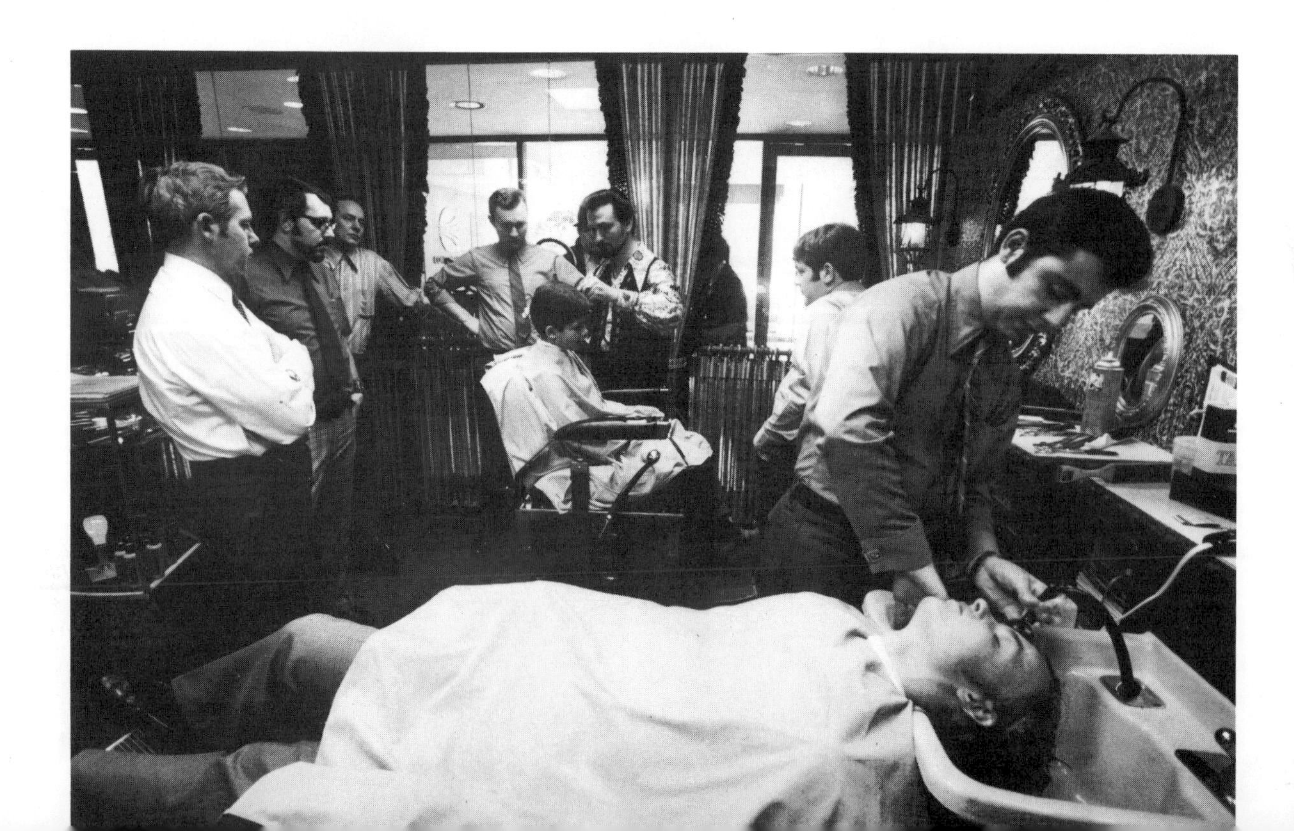

The Hancock's largest tenant is a department store. Its main entrance is on the lower concourse, and the entire store takes up five floors of space.

Most people who come to the Hancock get to ride on one of the five moving staircases, or escalators. The escalators take passengers from the concourses below street level to the second floor, where most of the Hancock's fifty elevators begin their long climbs.

On the second floor there usually is an exhibition of paintings or photographs. Starting from this floor, Lauren Baker, who lives on floor sixty-two, presses the button for the ninety-second floor to visit a friend after school. The elevator whisks her upstairs at more than twenty miles per hour!

Between the thirteenth and forty-first floors are more than 400 business offices, where all sorts of interesting work is done. On the twenty-seventh floor some television experts prepare a commercial. The Institute for Foreign Studies, on a nearby floor, helps a student choose a foreign college so that she can continue her education overseas.

Ira Brichta's advertising business is on the thirty-ninth floor. In a pleasant moment, Ira talks to a client about a new advertisement in which a model will wear a funny hat.

On the forty-third floor tremendous air-conditioning machines help to keep the temperature of the Hancock Center under perfect control all year 'round. Big John uses as much power as a city of 30,000 people. The building contains 1,250 miles of electrical wiring and has 11,459 panes of glass. If the glass were stretched out, it would measure thirteen miles in length and five feet in width.

The Hancock Center has its own police force and police station. The chief and his men use radios and walkie-talkies to communicate. One day they caught a man who had set five fires in the building. The policemen are always watching for people who try to sneak out of the building with typewriters or lamps.

trim line

The forty-fourth floor of Big John is the most unusual in the whole gigantic building. It has the world's highest supermarket and swimming pool–546 feet high.

The forty-fourth floor also has a sauna bath, a restaurant, and a mailroom-in-the-sky, where residents can collect letters and parcels sent up from the basement postal station.

The Hancock Center is the only building more than 100 stories high that has both offices and apartments. Lauren Baker and her brother Todd live in one of Big John's 705 apartments. Lauren's telescope came in handy for a homework report on Lake Michigan. The children's favorite sight? Looking *down* at helicopters from their sixty-second-story perch.

For fun, the Baker children sometimes go down to the thirty-ninth floor to visit their father in his office. But living in Big John is not *all* fun. Only one pet is allowed on each floor! The first family on the floor to move in with a pet gets to keep it. If the pet is small, it has to be carried in a canvas sling so that it won't soil the hall carpets.

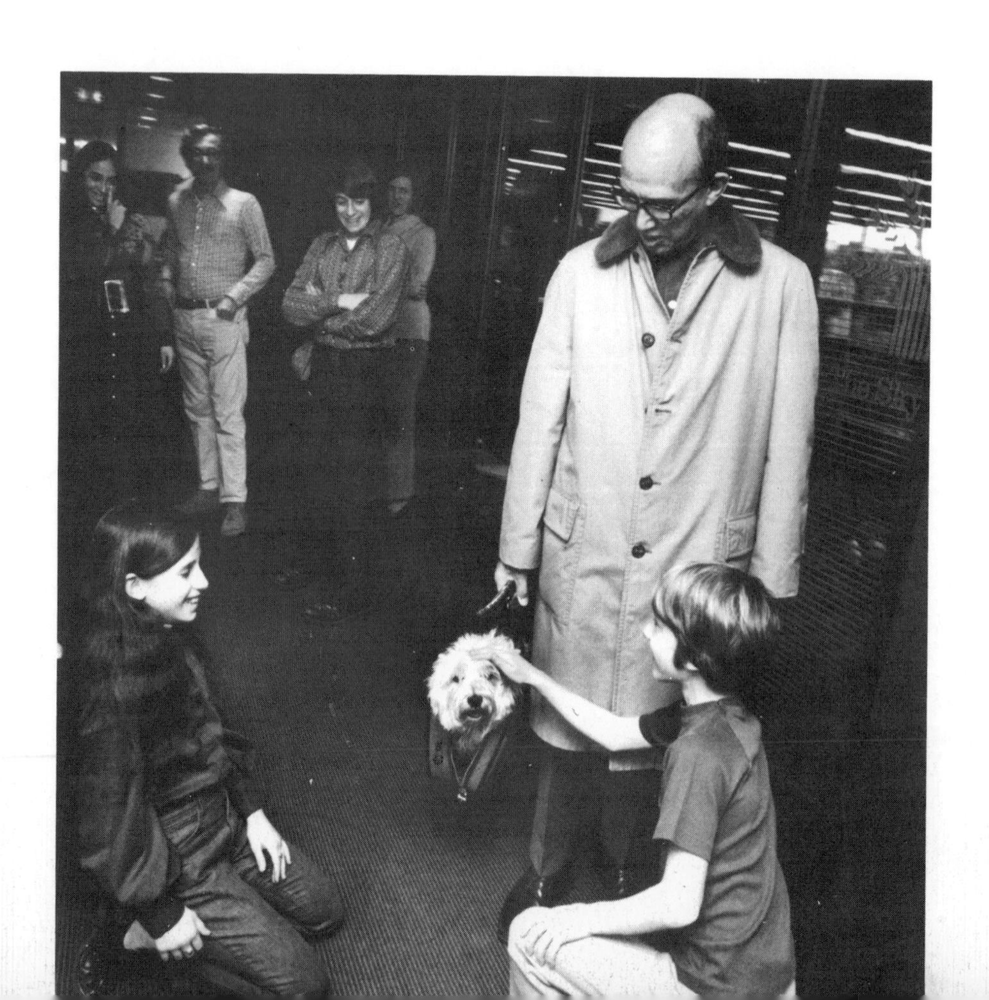

Children living in the Hancock Center can play hide-and-seek in a large lobby-in-the-sky. Todd's favorite hiding place is this crevice, formed by two of the huge beams that make up Big John's 46,000-ton steel framework. That's enough steel for 33,000 cars!

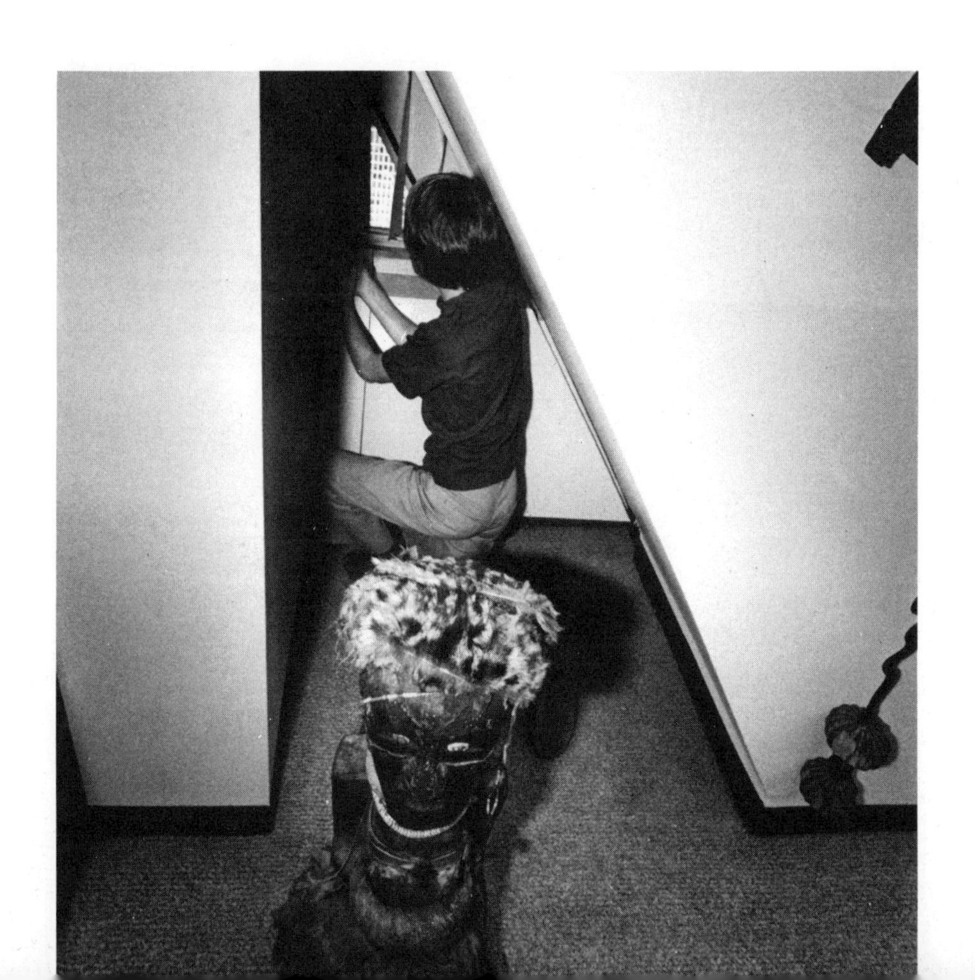

It took 2,000 men working 5 million man-hours to build Big John. Keeping Big John in good shape–or "maintaining" the building–takes more than 500 men and women: electricians, plumbers, carpenters, cleaning people, and window washers for all those windows. The window washers have one of the scariest maintenance jobs. They climb down from the roof of the building onto a moving platform that hangs from heavy cables, the way lifeboats hang down from the sides of big ships.

The window washers carry water tanks, soap, and squeegees. They squirt water at the windows–sometimes scaring the residents–and then wipe the water off. They love their work–except on very cold days, when their water starts to freeze. "It's not too good an idea to look down," says one window washer, "especially if you've just had your lunch."

The observatory is on the ninety-fourth floor, 1,030 feet above the ground. For a dime you can look through one of the twenty-four telescopes, and on a clear day you can see four states–Illinois, Indiana, Wisconsin, and Michigan. Michigan is more than sixty miles away. When the sun is right, Big John's shadow covers blocks and blocks of Chicago and even stretches out into Lake Michigan.

When the John Hancock Center was built, a sky capsule was placed in the observatory. The capsule will be opened in 100 years. It contains reels of movies, recordings, baseballs, and other objects our great-great-great-grandchildren may want to see. Of course, by then Big John may be just another *small* building.

On the ninety-fifth floor an expensive restaurant called "The 95th" has a breathtaking view of Chicago.

Most of Chicago's television and radio stations transmit their programs from the Hancock's two towers. Engineers work on the ninety-seventh floor to make sure that the pictures and sounds that the studios send to the Hancock over telephone wires are beamed out from the towers as clearly as possible.

During rush hours a traffic expert with a telescope checks on cars and broadcasts what he sees to drivers on their way home from work. He recommends routes that are the least crowded.

Big John never sleeps. At night the cleaning men and women prepare the offices and hallways for the next day's business. The maintenance people carefully check the many machines that make the Hancock Center a comfortable city-in-the-sky. In the apartments boys and girls finish their homework while their parents watch television – beamed down to them from their very own roof.